THE COURAGE TO HEAL

Empower Self-Healing, Break Free from Trauma, Recover & Rebuild Emotional Strength, and Achieve Lifelong Transformation

PREM SAGAR SUNCHU

YOUR FREE GIFT !!

As a token of my thanks for taking out time to read my book, I would like to offer you a **Free-Gift**:

Click the Below Link and Download your **Free eBook PDF**.

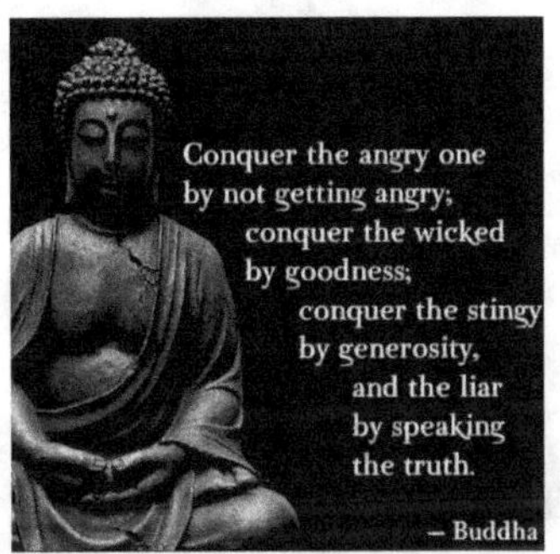

"The Power of Community: Thriving Together"

ABOUT THE AUTHOR

Prem Sagar Sunchu, the Accomplished Author of "The Courage To Heal"

Meet **Mr. Prem Sagar**, an ordinary soul born in the vibrant city of Secunderabad, India, where the tapestry of life weaves stories of resilience and dreams. His journey is a testament to the power of perpetual learning, where every encounter is a lesson, and every moment holds the potential for growth.

A man of many dimensions, Mr. Sagar embodies the qualities of a perpetual student, a dedicated listener, and a dreamer who gazes at the stars but keeps his feet firmly grounded. His aspirations soar high, and his relentless pursuit of them is fueled by a genuine desire to make a positive impact on those around him.

Having served as a Chief Manager in the prestigious State Bank of India, Mr. Sagar brings a wealth of experience from the world of banking. However, for him, retirement isn't a conclusion but a commencement—a reminder that life's true journey begins when one can reflect on the wisdom gained from the first innings.

In Mr. Sagar's view, retirement is not a retreat but a stepping stone to a realm of infinite possibilities. It's an opportunity to surpass the ordinary, where the canvas of life awaits new brushstrokes of creativity and purpose. For him, the "be good and do good policy" isn't just a mantra; it's a guiding principle that shapes his approach to life.

As he embraces the second innings, Mr. Sagar encourages others to view retirement not as a winding down but as a springboard to new endeavors. It's a time when accumulated wisdom meets fresh energy, and the monotony of routine gives way to the vibrancy of creativity. His belief is clear: retirement is not just a number; it's a chapter where the richness of experience meets the possibilities in abundance.

In the world of Mr. Prem Sagar, retirement is not a period of rest but a canvas waiting to be painted with the colors of newfound wisdom, creativity, and a different outlook on life.

Prem Sagar Sunchu
M.Com, LLM, Certified Independent Director (IICA)
GOI,
Author, Sole Arbitrator and Legal Consultant, Freelancer

ACKNOWLEDGEMENTS

In profound gratitude, I extend heartfelt appreciation to my amazing parents. To my caring and resilient mother, **Smt. S.L. Lakshmi**, who gracefully navigated the challenges of my father's service transfers, made countless sacrifices to bind our family together. My father, **Shri S.R. Lakshman Rao**, stands as my enduring role model—his post-retirement vibrancy, marked by a dedicated hobby of reading and writing, serves as the very foundation that propels me into the realm of authorship. A debt of gratitude is owed to my beautiful wife, **Smt. S.P. Padma Sree** is a constant source of inspiration, unwavering strength, and invaluable guidance. Balancing family responsibilities and the intricate path of an author, her presence has been the foundation of my journey.

To my handsome sons, **S.P. Gautam Sagar, S.P. Prayag Sagar**, and **S.P. Akshaj Sagar**, whose unwavering support and responsibility bear testament to the great strength they provide. Their motivation fuels my endeavors across all the diverse traits I undertake.

I owe thanks to **Mr. Som Bathla**, an **Amazon #1 Best-selling** author, for his mentorship, motivation, and guidance in the realms of **Writing, Self-Publishing, and Launching Books**. His support has been instrumental in initiating my journey as an Authorpreneur.

My Sincere thanks to **Mr. Sooraj Achar**, who is also an Amazon Bestselling Author, for his **Professional Editing**, Formatting, and Publishing support.

In acknowledging these pillars of support, I am reminded that the tapestry of my life and authorial pursuit is woven with threads of love, sacrifice, and inspiration. With profound thanks to my family, who stand as my bedrock of strength and motivation.

DEDICATION

To the guiding stars of my universe—my Parents, Grandparents, Parents-in-law, Brothers, Sisters, the cherished members of our extended Family and Friends. Their unwavering support and boundless encouragement have been the driving force behind my Author Journey.

In the tapestry of my life, each of them has woven threads of inspiration and resilience, transforming mere words into stories and dreams into realities. Their confidence in me has been a constant source of strength, propelling me forward through the path of this journey.

With heartfelt gratitude, I dedicate the pages of my work to the pillars of love and encouragement that they are, recognizing that every word I pen is a tribute to the collective spirit of our family. May this dedication reflect the depth of my appreciation for the profound impact they have had on my creative journey.

"The Courage To Heal" is my third book in the series of five books-"**The Resilient Mind."**

CONTENTS

EMBARK ON A TRANSFORMATIVE JOURNEY

Embark on a transformative journey with:

'The Courage To Heal'

"A ray of hope for those seeking liberation from the shackles of trauma. Discover the empowering wisdom to break free from the past, unlock your inner strength, and emerge resilient, renewed, and reborn. Through these pages, unlock the secrets to self-healing, shatter the chains of emotional pain, and rise into a life of purpose, joy, and unbridled potential – where every scar becomes a testament to your unyielding courage and every breath a celebration of your triumphant spirit."

THE JOURNEY OF HEALING

"Healing doesn't mean the damage never existed. It means the damage no longer controls our lives." — Unknown

Introduction:

Life can be both beautiful and challenging. Along the way, many of us accumulate emotional wounds—scars that affect our mental and emotional health, often in ways we may not even realize. Whether from relationships, trauma, loss, or other experiences, these emotional injuries can limit our ability to live freely and fully. This chapter explores what it takes to heal, the resilience needed to overcome these scars, and how you can reclaim control over your life.

Healing is not linear or simple. It requires strength, patience, and self-compassion. While everyone's journey is different, the key to overcoming emotional and psychological wounds lies in resilience—the ability to adapt, grow, and rise again despite the challenges. It takes courage to face these wounds, but the rewards of healing are immense: a renewed sense of self, freedom from past pain, and the opportunity to move forward with clarity and confidence.

Understanding Emotional Wounds: Defining Emotional and Psychological Scars

Emotional wounds are the deep, often invisible scars left by painful experiences. They may arise from childhood trauma, abusive relationships, the loss of a loved one, or even events that seem trivial to others but are profoundly significant to us. These wounds manifest in various ways: anxiety, depression, anger, fear of rejection, and difficulty trusting others.

One compelling case study is of *Sarah,* who, after the sudden death of her father, struggled for years with feelings of abandonment and anxiety. The emotional wound left her unable to form close relationships, afraid that others would leave her too. Through therapy and self-reflection, she began to understand that these fears were rooted in unresolved grief. She realized the need to process her emotions instead of letting them control her. Slowly, Sarah rebuilt her life, learning that while the pain of loss never truly fades, it doesn't have to define her future.

Psychological research underscores the long-lasting effects of untreated emotional trauma. A 2014 study by Van der Kolk revealed that unresolved trauma could leave individuals in a perpetual state of hyper-vigilance, where they are constantly anticipating danger, even when none is present. This heightened emotional state can impact every aspect of life—from personal relationships to professional achievements—making healing essential for overall well-being.

The Power of Resilience: Why Healing Requires Strength, Perseverance, and Courage

Resilience isn't about being invulnerable; it's about being able to recover. When we are emotionally wounded, it can feel like the end of the world. But resilience allows us to bounce back, adapt, and eventually thrive. Healing takes perseverance, and setbacks are inevitable. The process requires confronting pain, accepting vulnerability, and acknowledging the difficult emotions that come with it.

Consider *James,* a combat veteran who returned home with post-traumatic stress disorder (PTSD). His trauma was compounded by the guilt of surviving when some of his comrades did not. For years, James turned to alcohol to numb his feelings, distancing himself from his family and friends. But with the help of support groups and a therapist specializing in trauma, he gradually rebuilt his life. James learned coping strategies that allowed him to face his emotions rather than suppress them. He found strength in vulnerability and in sharing his story with others.

Scientific evidence supports this. A 2020 study in *Frontiers in Psychology* found that individuals with higher resilience levels are more likely to recover from trauma and maintain emotional stability. They engage in adaptive coping strategies, such as problem-solving and seeking social support, which are crucial in overcoming emotional challenges.

Reclaiming Your Life: The Role of Mindset in the Healing Process

Your mindset plays a crucial role in how effectively you heal. The way you view yourself, your experiences, and your future shapes your emotional journey. Cultivating a growth mindset—believing that you have the power to change and heal—can make all the difference. Healing is not about erasing the past but about transforming it. It involves accepting what has happened and making a conscious decision to move forward.

In Sarah's case, she discovered that her journey to healing began when she shifted from a victim mentality to an empowered one. Instead of asking, "Why did this happen to me?" she started asking, "What can I learn from this?" Her change in perspective was the first step in reclaiming control over her emotional health.

According to Carol Dweck's research on mindset, individuals with a growth mindset are more likely to overcome emotional wounds because they view challenges as opportunities for personal development. This mentality is critical for those who are on the journey to healing.

What You Will Discover: How This Book Will Guide You to Rebuild Mental and Emotional Health

This book serves as a roadmap for those looking to heal emotional and psychological scars. It offers practical strategies for developing resilience, rebuilding self-confidence, and reclaiming your life after hardship. Through a combination of research-based techniques and compelling case studies, you will learn how to face your wounds, understand their origins, and develop the strength needed to move forward.

You will also discover the power of mindset in shaping your healing journey, helping you to view setbacks as stepping stones rather than barriers. Healing is possible, and this book will guide you on that path.

Key Insights:

- **Emotional wounds** are invisible scars that impact mental health and personal relationships. Healing requires acknowledging and addressing these wounds.

- **Resilience** is the key to recovery. It involves the ability to adapt, persevere, and rise above adversity.

- **Mindset** plays a crucial role in the healing process. A growth mindset fosters emotional recovery, while a fixed mindset can hinder it.

- **Scientific evidence** supports the idea that resilience, social support, and adaptive coping strategies contribute to emotional healing.

Conclusion:

Healing emotional wounds takes time, effort, and courage, but it is possible for anyone willing to commit to the journey. Whether your pain stems from trauma, loss, or difficult relationships, you can reclaim control of your emotional well-being by embracing resilience and cultivating a mindset that promotes growth. The scars will remain, but they no longer have to define you. Through this journey, you will discover strength, clarity, and the freedom to live your life with renewed purpose.

Resources:

1. Van der Kolk, B. (2014). *The Body Keeps the Score: Brain, Mind, and Body in the Healing of Trauma.*

2. Dweck, C. S. (2006). *Mindset: The New Psychology of Success.*

3. *Frontiers in Psychology* (2020). "Resilience as a Moderator of the Relationship Between Trauma and Mental Health Outcomes."

4. Herman, J. (1992). *Trauma and Recovery: The Aftermath of Violence—from Domestic Abuse to Political Terror.*

5. National Institute of Mental Health. (2021). "Coping with Traumatic Events."

CHAPTER 1

FACING THE PAIN: CONFRONTING EMOTIONAL WOUNDS

"You can't heal what you refuse to acknowledge."
— Anonymous

Introduction:

Emotional pain is often invisible but profoundly real. Many people carry hidden wounds from past experiences—wounds that shape how they live, think, and relate to others. Healing requires more than time; it demands that you confront your pain head-on. This chapter is about recognizing those emotional wounds, breaking the cycle of denial, and shifting your mindset to see pain as an opportunity for growth. By understanding these concepts, you'll learn practical steps to begin the healing journey and rebuild your emotional well-being.

Acknowledging Your Struggles: The First Step to Healing is Recognition

Acknowledging emotional pain is an act of courage. Many people live in silent suffering, either unaware of the depth of their pain or too afraid to confront it. They may carry unresolved grief, anger, shame, or fear without ever fully recognizing the impact it has on their daily lives. This hidden pain can manifest as anxiety, depression, or emotional numbness, gradually eroding one's sense of self.

A case in point is *Rachel,* who, for years, struggled with an overwhelming sense of guilt after a breakup. She blamed herself for the relationship's failure, internalizing her pain and refusing to acknowledge how deeply it was affecting her mental health. She threw herself into work to distract herself, hoping the pain would fade. Instead, her anxiety worsened, and she felt increasingly isolated. It wasn't until she recognized and accepted her emotions that she began to heal. Acknowledgment allowed her to start processing her pain and to see it for what it was—an opportunity to learn and grow, not a permanent scar.

Research supports the importance of acknowledgment in emotional healing. A study published in *Emotion* (2015) found that individuals who actively process their negative emotions, rather than suppressing them, experience faster emotional recovery and lower levels of stress. The study suggests that the simple act of recognition is the foundation upon which healing is built.

Breaking the Cycle of Denial: How Avoiding Pain Delays Recovery

Denial can be a coping mechanism. When faced with deep emotional pain, it's easy to push it aside or pretend it doesn't exist. We often convince ourselves that ignoring the pain will make it disappear. But in reality, denial prolongs suffering. The more we avoid our emotions, the more they manifest in destructive ways—through unhealthy relationships, addiction, or physical symptoms such as headaches or fatigue.

Michael's story illustrates this. After losing his job unexpectedly, he felt a deep sense of failure. Rather than facing his feelings of inadequacy, he convinced himself that he didn't care about the job and pushed his emotions away. Over time, his denial manifested in irritability and emotional withdrawal from his family. It was only when his marriage began to suffer that Michael realized he needed to confront the loss and the emotions he had buried. Once he acknowledged the grief, he was able to start rebuilding his life and self-esteem.

Psychological research shows that avoidance behaviors, such as denial, are linked to higher levels of emotional distress over time. A 2016 study in the *Journal of Behavioral Therapy* demonstrated that individuals who avoided confronting painful emotions were more likely to experience anxiety, depression, and prolonged psychological stress. Breaking the cycle of denial is a critical step in recovery, allowing individuals to face the underlying issues and begin healing.

Shifting Your Perspective: Viewing Pain as a Catalyst for Growth

Pain can be transformative if we allow it to be. While it's natural to want to avoid suffering, emotional pain often carries valuable lessons. It can force us to examine our lives, our choices, and our beliefs in ways that we might not have otherwise. Instead of seeing pain as something to avoid, what if we saw it as a tool for growth?

Angela experienced this shift after a period of severe burnout at her corporate job. The stress was overwhelming, and for years she viewed it as a sign of personal failure. It wasn't until she reframed her perspective that things began to change. Instead of seeing her emotional exhaustion as weakness, she started seeing it as a signal—an indication that her life was out of balance. Angela began making changes to her work-life balance and investing in her emotional well-being, using the pain as a wake-up call to realign her life with her values.

This mindset shift is supported by research. According to a study in the *Journal of Personality and Social Psychology* (2019), individuals who view adversity as an opportunity for growth are more likely to experience positive psychological changes after stressful events. This phenomenon, known as post-traumatic growth, illustrates that even painful experiences can contribute to greater emotional resilience and personal development.

Practical Steps to Begin Healing: Journaling, Therapy, and Mindfulness

Healing is not an abstract concept—it involves practical, daily actions that help you process and release emotional pain. Three powerful tools that can facilitate this process are journaling, therapy, and mindfulness.

1. **Journaling** is a way to give your emotions a voice. Writing down your thoughts and feelings allows you to reflect on your experiences in a safe, private space. Research has shown that journaling can improve emotional clarity and reduce symptoms of depression. It allows you to process your emotions rather than keeping them bottled up, making it easier to understand and address your pain.

2. **Therapy** provides a structured environment where you can explore your emotional wounds with the guidance of a trained professional. Cognitive-behavioral therapy (CBT) has been particularly effective in helping individuals reframe negative thoughts and challenge unhelpful beliefs about themselves. Therapy offers a space for validation and growth, where

you can confront your pain with support and guidance.

3. **Mindfulness** teaches you to stay present with your emotions without judgment. Instead of avoiding or overanalyzing your pain, mindfulness encourages you to observe your feelings as they are, without trying to change them. Studies published in the *Journal of Clinical Psychology* suggest that mindfulness-based practices can reduce emotional reactivity and promote greater emotional stability.

Each of these methods offers a different but complementary approach to healing. Together, they create a foundation for confronting emotional pain in a way that leads to growth and recovery.

Key Insights:

- Acknowledging emotional wounds is the first and most crucial step toward healing.

- Denial only delays recovery, allowing emotional pain to manifest in harmful ways.

- Shifting your perspective on pain can transform it into a catalyst for growth and personal development.

- Practical steps, such as journaling, therapy, and mindfulness, provide essential tools for emotional healing.

Conclusion:

Facing emotional wounds is daunting, but it's the only path to true healing. Denying or avoiding pain only prolongs the suffering, while acknowledging it allows for processing and eventual release. By shifting your mindset, you can view pain as a potential for growth, turning difficult experiences into opportunities for resilience and transformation. Healing is a journey—one that begins with recognition and continues through active, daily steps toward emotional well-being.

Resources:

1. *Emotion* (2015). "Processing Negative Emotions: A Pathway to Emotional Recovery."

2. Journal of Behavioral Therapy (2016). "The Role of Avoidance in Prolonging Emotional Distress."

3. *Journal of Personality and Social Psychology* (2019). "Post-Traumatic Growth: The Benefits of Adversity."

4. Pennebaker, J. (1997). *Opening Up: The Healing Power of Expressing Emotions.*

5. National Institute of Mental Health. (2022). "Cognitive-Behavioral Therapy for Emotional Health."

CHAPTER 2

BUILDING EMOTIONAL RESILIENCE

"Life doesn't get easier or more forgiving; we get stronger and more resilient." — Steve Maraboli

Introduction:

Emotional resilience is what enables individuals to bounce back from adversity, adapt to change, and keep moving forward despite life's challenges. It isn't about being unaffected by hardships—it's about developing the inner strength to recover, learn, and thrive after difficult experiences. This chapter explores what emotional resilience truly is, how to cultivate a resilient mindset, daily strategies for strengthening emotional resilience, and how to view setbacks as opportunities for growth.

What is Emotional Resilience? Understanding the Key Components

Emotional resilience refers to the ability to adapt to stressful situations, emotional upheavals, and crises in a way that preserves one's mental and emotional health. It doesn't mean never feeling pain or hardship; rather, it's about maintaining balance and finding ways to cope effectively, even under pressure. There are several key components to emotional resilience, including:

- **Emotional regulation:** The capacity to manage and control emotional reactions rather than being overwhelmed by them.

- **Optimism:** A general belief that things will improve, allowing individuals to keep hope alive even during tough times.

- **Support systems:** The presence of people—whether friends, family, or professionals—who provide emotional support and understanding.

- **Self-efficacy:** A strong belief in one's own ability to solve problems and handle challenges.

Take the case of *David,* a small business owner who faced bankruptcy after an economic downturn. Instead of succumbing to despair, David demonstrated emotional resilience. He managed his fear and anxiety through mindfulness, maintained his optimism by focusing on future opportunities, and leaned on his support network. As a result, not only did he avoid falling into deep depression, but he also developed new business strategies that allowed him to rebuild his company successfully.

Research from the American Psychological Association (2020) indicates that emotional resilience is not an inherent trait but a skill that can be developed over time. By focusing on key areas like emotional regulation and social support, individuals can build resilience that serves them in times of difficulty.

Developing a Resilient Mindset: Shifting from Victimhood to Empowerment

A resilient mindset shifts the focus from victimhood—where one feels helpless in the face of adversity—to empowerment, where challenges are seen as opportunities for growth. This shift involves changing the way we perceive setbacks, moving from a place of defeat to one of determination and personal responsibility.

Maria's story is a testament to this transformation. After enduring a painful divorce, she initially felt victimized by her circumstances. Her self-esteem plummeted, and she struggled to see a future without her former spouse. However, through therapy and self-reflection, Maria began to reclaim her sense of agency. She realized that while she couldn't change the past, she had control over her future. Maria started setting personal goals, rediscovered her passions, and built a new life around the things that mattered to her. Her shift from feeling powerless to empowered enabled her to rebuild her life on her terms.

Research supports the importance of mindset in resilience. A 2016 study in the *Journal of Positive Psychology* found that individuals who adopt a "challenge" mindset—seeing adversity as an opportunity to grow—are more likely to experience positive outcomes after difficult events. This mindset not only helps individuals cope with stress but also encourages personal development.

Strategies for Strengthening Emotional Muscles: Daily Habits for Resilience

Building emotional resilience requires daily effort and intentional practice. Like physical muscles, emotional resilience grows stronger with regular exercise. Here are a few strategies to develop emotional "muscles":

1. **Mindfulness meditation:** Practicing mindfulness allows you to stay present with your emotions without being consumed by them. Mindfulness enhances emotional regulation, helping you manage stress more effectively.

2. **Gratitude journaling:** Writing down what you are thankful for can shift your perspective from focusing on problems to recognizing the good in your life. This fosters a sense of optimism and reduces negative

emotions.

3. **Physical exercise:** Engaging in regular physical activity improves mood and lowers stress levels. Exercise triggers the release of endorphins, which are natural mood boosters that can help combat anxiety and depression.

4. **Seeking social support:** Building strong, supportive relationships is essential for resilience. Social support provides emotional validation and practical assistance during difficult times, enhancing one's ability to cope.

Scientific studies back the efficacy of these strategies. For example, a 2019 review in *Psychiatry Research* found that individuals who practiced mindfulness regularly had significantly higher levels of emotional resilience and were better able to cope with stress than those who didn't. Similarly, gratitude has been linked to increased psychological well-being, fostering greater resilience in the face of adversity.

Bouncing Back from Setbacks: Turning Failures into Opportunities for Growth

Setbacks and failures are an inevitable part of life, but how we respond to them is what makes the difference. Rather than viewing failures as the end of the road, resilient individuals see them as opportunities for learning and growth. This mindset allows them to bounce back stronger, armed with new insights and strategies for future success.

Consider *Jake,* an aspiring athlete who, after suffering a severe injury, was told he might never compete again. Instead of giving up, Jake shifted his focus. He used the time to strengthen other areas of his body and worked with his doctors to craft a recovery plan. Although the injury temporarily sidelined him, Jake eventually returned to his sport with a deeper appreciation for his body and a more focused training regimen. The setback, rather than ending his career, became a turning point for personal growth.

Research highlights this principle. A study in *Personality and Social Psychology Bulletin* (2017) revealed that individuals who view setbacks as learning experiences are more likely to exhibit resilience. The study found that adopting a growth mindset—where challenges are embraced as opportunities to improve—leads to greater emotional stability and perseverance.

Key Insights:

- Emotional resilience is the ability to adapt, recover, and grow from adversity.

- Developing a resilient mindset requires shifting from victimhood to empowerment, focusing on personal agency and growth.

- Strengthening emotional resilience involves daily practices like mindfulness, gratitude journaling, exercise, and seeking social support.

- Setbacks can be transformed into opportunities for growth with the right perspective, allowing individuals to bounce back stronger.

Conclusion:

Building emotional resilience isn't about avoiding challenges—it's about developing the inner strength to face them head-on and come out stronger. By understanding what emotional resilience is and actively practicing strategies to strengthen it, you can develop the capacity to not only survive adversity but thrive because of it. With resilience, every setback becomes an opportunity for growth, every failure a chance to learn, and every hardship a stepping stone toward personal empowerment.

Resources:

1. American Psychological Association (2020). "The Road to Resilience."

2. Journal of Positive Psychology (2016). "The Role of Mindset in Coping with Adversity."

3. *Psychiatry Research* (2019). "Mindfulness and Emotional Resilience: A Review of the Literature."

4. Personality and Social Psychology Bulletin (2017). "Embracing Failure: How a Growth Mindset Promotes Emotional Resilience."

5. Kabat-Zinn, J. (1994). *Wherever You Go, There You Are: Mindfulness Meditation in Everyday Life.*

CHAPTER 3

HEALING THROUGH FORGIVENESS

"Forgiveness is not an occasional act; it is a constant attitude." — Martin Luther King Jr.

Introduction:

Forgiveness is often misunderstood as an act of weakness or a gesture for the benefit of others, but in reality, it's one of the most powerful tools for personal healing. Holding onto grudges, anger, or guilt traps us in the past, hindering our emotional growth. This chapter delves into the transformative power of forgiveness, why it's essential for both personal freedom and mental well-being, and how to apply forgiveness in our lives. Through understanding, self-compassion, and practical exercises, you'll learn how to forgive yourself and others, fostering inner peace in the process.

Understanding the Power of Forgiveness: How Releasing Grudges Sets You Free

Forgiveness is often portrayed as a gift we give to others, but in reality, it's a gift we give to ourselves. Holding on to resentment and anger is emotionally exhausting, keeping us chained to past events that cannot be undone. Studies have shown that refusing to forgive contributes to higher stress levels, worsened mental health, and can even manifest in physical symptoms like headaches and insomnia.

Jessica's experience illustrates the transformative power of forgiveness. After a bitter argument with her sister that led to years of estrangement, Jessica found herself consumed with anger and regret. She replayed the argument in her head, wondering why her sister couldn't see her side of things. It wasn't until she attended a personal development workshop on forgiveness that Jessica realized she was the one suffering most from holding onto the grudge. She decided to forgive her sister, not because she felt her actions were justified, but because she deserved peace. Forgiveness freed her from the emotional prison she had been living in for years.

Psychological research supports this. A 2001 study published in *The Journal of Behavioral Medicine* found that individuals who practice forgiveness report lower levels of anxiety, depression, and anger, and higher levels of emotional well-being. Forgiveness is not about erasing the past, but rather about reclaiming control over your emotions and moving forward with clarity.

Forgiving Yourself and Others: Techniques to Let Go of Guilt and Resentment

Forgiveness begins with the self. Often, the hardest person to forgive is yourself. Whether due to past mistakes, regrets, or perceived failures, holding onto self-blame keeps you stuck in a cycle of guilt and shame. Learning to forgive yourself is a critical step toward healing.

Tom struggled with feelings of guilt for years after his business venture failed, leaving him in debt and feeling like a disappointment to his family. He couldn't forgive himself for what he saw as personal failure, and the guilt weighed heavily on him, affecting his self-worth and relationships. With the help of therapy, Tom learned to view the failure as a learning experience rather than a reflection of his character. He practiced self-compassion exercises and gradually let go of the guilt, realizing that he had done his best with the knowledge and resources available at the time.

Forgiving others, too, is essential, even when they haven't apologized or acknowledged the harm they've caused. Holding onto resentment allows the other person to maintain power over your emotions. By letting go of that resentment, you reclaim your emotional freedom. Techniques like writing forgiveness letters (which you don't necessarily have to send) or guided meditations can help in this process.

Research shows that self-forgiveness is correlated with higher psychological well-being and reduced stress. A 2012 study published in the *Journal of Health Psychology* found that those who practiced self-forgiveness had better health outcomes and more positive emotional experiences, emphasizing that releasing guilt and resentment is crucial for overall wellness.

Healing Isn't Linear: Embracing the Ups and Downs of the Forgiveness Process

Forgiveness, like healing, is not a one-time event. It's a process with highs and lows. You may forgive someone today but feel the sting of the past tomorrow. That doesn't mean you've failed; it simply means that healing takes time. Embracing the nonlinear nature of forgiveness is part of the journey.

Lina's experience of healing after an emotionally abusive relationship took years. She would feel at peace one day, convinced she had fully forgiven her ex-partner, only to be triggered by a small memory the next. Initially, she felt frustrated by the emotional rollercoaster, thinking she hadn't made progress. But over time, Lina realized that healing through forgiveness is a gradual process. With every wave of emotions, she grew stronger and more self-aware, eventually reaching a place of lasting peace.

Research published in *Personality and Social Psychology Bulletin* (2016) emphasizes that forgiveness is a dynamic process that involves repeated cycles of emotional release and personal growth. The key is to remain patient and compassionate with yourself throughout the journey, acknowledging that setbacks are a natural part of progress.

Forgiveness Practices: Guided Exercises to Foster Inner Peace

Practicing forgiveness requires more than intellectual understanding—it involves daily action. Here are some effective techniques to help you on your path to forgiveness:

1. **Forgiveness Letter:** Write a letter to someone who has hurt you, or even to yourself. Express your feelings honestly, but conclude the letter by consciously choosing to forgive. You don't have to send the letter; it's more about releasing the emotions tied to the situation.

2. **Self-Forgiveness Affirmations:** Create and repeat affirmations focused on self-compassion and forgiveness, such as "I forgive myself for past mistakes. I am human, and I am learning." Affirmations help rewire negative thought patterns and cultivate a sense of self-worth.

3. **Loving-Kindness Meditation:** This form of med-

itation involves directing loving thoughts toward yourself, a loved one, a neutral person, and even someone you find difficult. By wishing them peace and happiness, you gradually dissolve feelings of resentment and anger.

4. **Visualization:** Close your eyes and imagine yourself setting down a heavy load that represents the anger or guilt you've been carrying. Visualize yourself walking away, lighter and free from the emotional baggage.

Scientific evidence supports the effectiveness of these practices. A 2018 study in *Frontiers in Psychology* found that individuals who engaged in forgiveness practices, such as loving-kindness meditation and writing exercises, experienced significant improvements in emotional well-being and stress reduction. Forgiveness is an active practice, and these exercises can help cultivate inner peace over time.

Key Insights:

- Forgiveness is not just a gift for others but a powerful tool for personal freedom and emotional healing.

- Self-forgiveness is a crucial first step in the process, as it helps release guilt and shame that may be hindering your growth.

- The process of forgiveness is not linear; it involves ups and downs that require patience and self-compassion.

- Guided exercises, such as forgiveness letters, affirmations, and meditation, can foster lasting inner peace and emotional resilience.

Conclusion:

Healing through forgiveness requires letting go of grudges, guilt, and resentment that weigh down your emotional well-being. While it can be a difficult journey, forgiveness offers the opportunity to release the past and embrace a more peaceful, empowered future. Whether forgiving yourself or others, the act of forgiveness is a profound step toward healing, inner peace, and freedom.

Resources:

1. Journal of Behavioral Medicine (2001). "Forgiveness and Mental Health: A Review of the Literature."

2. Journal of Health Psychology (2012). "The Role of Self-Forgiveness in Emotional and Physical Well-Being."

3. Personality and Social Psychology Bulletin (2016). "Forgiveness as a Nonlinear Process: Understanding the Dynamic Nature of Emotional Release."

4. *Frontiers in Psychology* (2018). "The Impact of Forgiveness Practices on Emotional Health and Stress."

5. Luskin, F. (2002). *Forgive for Good: A Proven Prescription for Health and Happiness.*

CHAPTER 4

CULTIVATING SELF-COMPASSION AND ACCEPTANCE

"You yourself, as much as anybody in the entire universe, deserve your love and affection." — Buddha

Introduction:

Self-compassion is the foundation of emotional well-being and healing. Often, people are their own harshest critics, holding themselves to unrealistic standards of perfection. This inner dialogue can hinder emotional recovery and amplify feelings of inadequacy. However, when we learn to practice self-compassion, we cultivate a healing environment within ourselves. This chapter explores the importance of self-love, the power of accepting imperfections, the role of gratitude in the healing process, and practical strategies to incorporate self-compassion into daily life.

The Importance of Self-Love: How Self-Compassion Accelerates Healing

Self-love is not selfish; it's essential for healing. When we practice self-compassion, we treat ourselves with kindness in moments of failure, pain, or inadequacy, rather than engaging in self-criticism. This inner kindness helps us recover from emotional wounds more quickly because it reduces stress and fosters a sense of safety within ourselves.

Lauren struggled with low self-esteem for most of her life. After being laid off from her job, she spiraled into self-criticism, blaming herself for her perceived failures. Her negative inner dialogue exacerbated her anxiety and depression. Eventually, Lauren began therapy, where she learned about self-compassion. By practicing daily affirmations and mindfulness exercises, she gradually shifted her perspective. Instead of berating herself for the layoff, she learned to view it as a part of life's ups and downs. This shift allowed her to recover emotionally, find a new job, and regain confidence.

Research highlights the connection between self-compassion and emotional recovery. A 2011 study in the *Journal of Clinical Psychology* found that individuals who practiced self-compassion experienced lower levels of anxiety and depression and were more resilient when faced with setbacks. Self-love creates the emotional space needed for healing, enabling individuals to move forward without being held back by self-judgment.

Embracing Your Imperfections: Accepting Yourself as You Are

Nobody is perfect, yet society often pushes unrealistic standards that leave people feeling inadequate. Learning to embrace your imperfections is a critical step toward cultivating self-compassion. When you accept yourself as you are, with all your flaws and mistakes, you release the pressure to be perfect, allowing more room for growth and healing.

Michael's journey of self-acceptance began after years of battling an eating disorder. He constantly felt ashamed of his appearance, and no matter how hard he tried to meet society's ideals, he always fell short. Through a support group, Michael learned that true healing would only begin when he accepted himself, imperfections and all. By practicing self-compassion, he started to see his body as a source of strength rather than an object to be criticized. Over time, Michael found peace with his body and built a healthier relationship with food and self-image.

Scientific evidence supports the importance of self-acceptance in emotional well-being. A 2017 study published in *Personality and Individual Differences* found that individuals who embraced their imperfections reported higher levels of life satisfaction and emotional stability. Accepting yourself doesn't mean settling for less; it means recognizing that your worth isn't dependent on perfection.

The Role of Gratitude in Healing: Focusing on Positive Aspects to Enhance Emotional Well-Being

Gratitude is a powerful tool for healing, helping to shift focus from what's wrong in life to what's going right. By practicing gratitude, you train your mind to appreciate the positive aspects of your life, even during challenging times. This shift in perspective enhances emotional resilience and cultivates a sense of inner peace.

Jessica experienced the benefits of gratitude while recovering from a serious illness. The diagnosis had left her feeling overwhelmed and anxious about the future. At the suggestion of her therapist, she began a gratitude journal, writing down three things she was grateful for each day, no matter how small. Over time, Jessica noticed a shift in her mindset. Instead of focusing solely on her health challenges, she began appreciating the support of her loved ones, the beauty of nature, and small joys in her daily life. Gratitude helped her maintain emotional balance, even in the face of uncertainty.

Research supports the link between gratitude and emotional well-being. A 2015 study in *Applied Psychology: Health and Well-Being* found that individuals who practiced gratitude regularly reported higher levels of happiness, lower stress, and improved physical health. Gratitude rewires the brain to focus on positive experiences, promoting emotional healing and resilience.

Practical Tips for Practicing Self-Compassion: Daily Exercises and Affirmations

Cultivating self-compassion requires consistent practice. Here are some simple but effective strategies to incorporate self-love into your daily routine:

1. **Self-Compassion Breaks:** Take a moment during stressful situations to pause and offer yourself words of kindness. Say things like, "This is hard, but I'm doing my best," or "I deserve kindness, even when things go wrong." These breaks help reduce the intensity of negative emotions and promote self-kindness in difficult moments.

2. **Daily Affirmations:** Write or say positive affirmations each morning, such as "I am worthy of love and compassion," or "I accept myself just as I am." These statements help reprogram negative thought patterns and encourage a more compassionate inner dialogue.

3. **Gratitude Journaling:** Keep a journal where you write down three things you are grateful for each day.

This practice shifts your focus from what's missing in your life to what's abundant, cultivating a positive and resilient mindset.

4. **Mindful Self-Compassion Meditation:** Spend a few minutes each day practicing mindfulness meditation with a focus on self-compassion. As you breathe deeply, silently repeat phrases like, "May I be kind to myself," or "May I find peace and healing." Mindfulness meditation helps you stay present and connected to your emotions without judgment.

5. **Embrace Self-Reflection:** Reflect on your thoughts and behaviors, not to criticize yourself, but to understand your patterns and how you can improve. Be gentle in your assessments and focus on progress rather than perfection.

A 2018 study in *Frontiers in Psychology* showed that mindfulness-based practices, such as meditation and self-compassion exercises, significantly increased emotional resilience and reduced negative self-talk. Incorporating these practices into daily life can help foster a more compassionate and accepting relationship with yourself.

Key Insights:

- Self-compassion is essential for emotional healing, reducing stress and fostering a positive inner dialogue.

- Accepting your imperfections allows you to grow and heal without the unrealistic pressure of perfectionism.

- Gratitude is a powerful tool for emotional resilience, helping you focus on the positive aspects of life even during tough times.

- Daily self-compassion exercises, such as affirmations, journaling, and mindfulness meditation, can help cultivate a more loving and peaceful relationship with yourself.

Conclusion:

Cultivating self-compassion and acceptance is a lifelong practice that accelerates healing and enhances emotional well-being. By embracing your imperfections and focusing on self-love, you create a nurturing space within yourself for growth, peace, and resilience. With practical tools like gratitude journaling, affirmations, and mindful self-compassion exercises, you can integrate self-love into your daily life, setting the foundation for emotional healing and acceptance.

Resources:

1. Neff, K. (2011). *Self-Compassion: The Proven Power of Being Kind to Yourself.*

2. Journal of Clinical Psychology (2011). "The Impact of Self-Compassion on Emotional Well-Being."

3. Personality and Individual Differences (2017). "Self-Acceptance and Life Satisfaction: Understanding the Correlation."

4. Applied Psychology: Health and Well-Being (2015). "Gratitude and Its Positive Effects on Health and Emotional Stability."

5. Frontiers in Psychology (2018). "The Benefits of Mindfulness and Self-Compassion Practices on Emotional Resilience."

CHAPTER 5

OVERCOMING FEAR AND REBUILDING TRUST

"Fear is the enemy of trust. Only by confronting fear can we build trust again." — Unknown

Introduction:

Fear and trust are closely intertwined, particularly in the process of emotional healing. Fear often arises after experiencing betrayal, loss, or trauma, and it can keep you from moving forward. Trust, on the other hand, is the foundation of healthy relationships—with yourself and others. This chapter explores the role fear plays in the healing process, the steps you can take to rebuild trust in yourself and others, how to create environments that promote safety, and techniques to restore confidence and a sense of security.

The Nature of Fear in Healing: Why Fear Holds You Back and How to Face It

Fear is a natural response to pain and trauma, and it's often the biggest barrier to healing. After being hurt, it's common to develop a fear of being vulnerable again. Whether it's the fear of being betrayed, abandoned, or judged, this emotion can keep you in a state of emotional paralysis, preventing you from opening up or trusting others.

Consider *Samantha,* who, after experiencing a deep betrayal by a close friend, found herself withdrawing from other relationships. Fear kept her from forming new connections because she didn't want to risk being hurt again. Over time, her social life dwindled, and she became increasingly isolated. It wasn't until Samantha acknowledged her fear and recognized how it was controlling her behavior that she could begin healing. By facing her fear head-on through therapy and small steps toward rebuilding relationships, Samantha learned to trust again.

Research underscores how fear impacts emotional healing. A study published in *Psychological Science* (2014) revealed that fear activates the brain's amygdala, triggering a fight-or-flight response that can lead to avoidance behaviors. This pattern reinforces fear, making it harder to heal unless it is consciously addressed. Facing fear with intention is the first step toward breaking free from its grip.

Rebuilding Trust in Yourself and Others: Steps to Open Your Heart Again

Trust, once broken, is difficult to rebuild, but it's not impossible. Rebuilding trust starts with yourself. After experiencing trauma or betrayal, many people lose confidence in their own judgment or abilities, questioning their worth or the choices they've made. To open your heart again, you first need to restore trust in yourself.

Ryan struggled with self-trust after going through a difficult breakup. He blamed himself for not seeing the red flags in the relationship, and his self-esteem plummeted. Every decision felt uncertain, and he hesitated to put himself out there again. Through self-reflection, therapy, and journaling, Ryan began to reconnect with his inner voice. He set small goals for himself, building confidence in his ability to make sound decisions. As Ryan rebuilt trust in himself, he found it easier to open up to others and develop new, healthier relationships.

Steps to rebuild trust include:

1. **Self-compassion:** Be kind to yourself as you navigate the rebuilding process. Understand that mistakes are part of life and that your past choices don't define your future.

2. **Set small goals:** Start with manageable steps that help restore confidence, such as rebuilding routines or making small commitments to others.

3. **Communicate openly:** When restoring trust with others, clear and honest communication is key. Express your feelings, fears, and expectations, and encourage open dialogue to build mutual understanding.

According to a 2015 study in the *Journal of Social and Personal Relationships*, self-trust is the cornerstone of rebuilding relationships with others. When individuals feel confident in their own decisions, they are more likely to engage in healthy, trusting relationships.

Creating Safe Spaces: Surrounding Yourself with Supportive People

Healing cannot happen in isolation. To overcome fear and rebuild trust, you need a safe environment—a space where you can be vulnerable, express your emotions, and feel understood without judgment. Surrounding yourself with supportive people helps create this environment.

Hannah had long-standing trust issues after growing up in a dysfunctional family. She was reluctant to share her thoughts and feelings, even with those close to her, because she feared being dismissed or ridiculed. It wasn't until Hannah joined a support group for individuals healing from family trauma that she found a safe space to open up. The understanding and empathy she received in that group helped her lower her emotional guard and begin healing.

Creating safe spaces doesn't just involve finding the right people; it also means setting boundaries and advocating for your emotional needs. It's okay to limit interactions with individuals who trigger anxiety or make you feel unsafe. Instead, focus on cultivating relationships where you feel respected, valued, and secure.

Research shows that social support plays a vital role in emotional recovery. A 2018 study in *Personality and Social Psychology Review* found that individuals who had access to emotionally supportive environments experienced faster healing from trauma and were more likely to rebuild trust in others. This sense of safety fosters emotional openness and the ability to engage in deeper, more authentic relationships.

Techniques for Restoring Confidence: How to Cultivate a Sense of Security Within

Rebuilding confidence after fear and betrayal is a process that involves internal and external work. Confidence comes from within, but it also requires consistent action to strengthen your belief in yourself. Here are a few techniques to restore your sense of security and rebuild confidence:

1. **Mindfulness Practice:** Mindfulness helps you stay grounded and connected to the present moment, reducing the influence of fear over your thoughts. Practicing mindfulness meditation or deep breathing exercises can help calm anxiety and build emo-

tional resilience.

2. **Positive Self-Talk:** Replace negative self-talk with affirmations that reinforce your worth and abilities. Statements like, "I am capable of making wise decisions," or "I trust myself to handle challenges," help shift your mindset and strengthen self-belief.

3. **Visualization:** Imagine yourself as confident, calm, and secure. Visualization techniques can help reframe your mind and create a mental picture of success, which boosts emotional confidence.

4. **Body Language:** How you carry yourself physically impacts your confidence. Practice standing tall, making eye contact, and engaging in assertive body language to reinforce an inner sense of security.

5. **Self-Care:** Engage in activities that make you feel empowered and in control, whether it's exercising, practicing a hobby, or simply taking time to rest and recharge. Self-care reinforces your commitment to yourself and builds trust in your own ability to nurture your emotional health.

A 2020 study in *Psychological Reports* demonstrated that individuals who practiced self-care and mindfulness techniques experienced a significant increase in self-confidence and emotional security. These techniques help individuals regain control over their internal world, fostering resilience in the face of challenges.

Key Insights:

- Fear, while natural, can block emotional healing and hinder trust. Facing it head-on is essential for growth.

- Rebuilding trust starts with yourself. By restoring confidence in your own decisions, you can open your heart to others.

- Surrounding yourself with supportive people and creating safe spaces promotes healing and fosters emotional security.

- Techniques such as mindfulness, positive self-talk, and visualization are practical ways to restore confidence and overcome fear.

Conclusion:

Overcoming fear and rebuilding trust requires courage, patience, and the right support systems. Fear keeps you in the past, but by confronting it and taking steps to rebuild trust in yourself and others, you can move forward with a renewed sense of security. Cultivating safe spaces and practicing techniques that enhance confidence will help you regain control over your emotions, rebuild trust, and open yourself to the possibility of deeper, healthier relationships.

Resources:

1. Psychological Science (2014). "The Role of Fear in Emotional Regulation and Avoidance Behavior."

2. Journal of Social and Personal Relationships (2015). "Self-Trust and Its Impact on Building Healthy Relationships."

3. Personality and Social Psychology Review (2018). "Social Support and Its Role in Emotional Healing and Trust-Building."

4. Psychological Reports (2020). "Mindfulness and

Self-Care as Tools for Rebuilding Confidence and Emotional Security."

5. Brown, B. (2012). *Daring Greatly: How the Courage to Be Vulnerable Transforms the Way We Live, Love, Parent, and Lead.*

CHAPTER 6

MOVING FORWARD WITH PURPOSE

"Healing is the key that unlocks the door to rediscovering your purpose and moving forward with clarity." — Unknown

Introduction:

Healing is a transformative process. As you heal from emotional wounds, you gain clarity about who you are, what you want, and where you're headed. Often, emotional pain clouds our sense of purpose and direction, leaving us feeling lost or disconnected from our goals. But once you've worked through that pain, the door opens to a new sense of purpose. This chapter focuses on how healing helps you redefine your path, the importance of setting new goals for personal growth, embracing the changes that come with newfound strength, and acknowledging that healing is a continuous journey.

Redefining Your Life's Path: How Healing Helps You Rediscover Purpose

Healing brings with it a sense of renewal. As you shed emotional baggage and break free from the chains of past hurts, you often begin to see life with a fresh perspective. Healing not only repairs what was broken but also enables you to rediscover what truly matters. It helps you connect with your authentic self—your desires, passions, and purpose.

Julia had spent years feeling unfulfilled in her career, though she couldn't pinpoint why. After overcoming the emotional toll of a divorce, she experienced a major shift in how she viewed her life. Through her healing process, Julia realized that she had pursued her career path more out of obligation than passion. With a clearer mind and a healed heart, she started exploring other possibilities that resonated more with her authentic self. Rediscovering her passion for art, Julia changed careers and found deep fulfillment in pursuing a creative path that aligned with her values and interests.

Psychological research supports this link between healing and rediscovery of purpose. A 2019 study published in *The Journal of Positive Psychology* showed that individuals who have undergone significant emotional healing are more likely to reassess their life's direction and identify new, meaningful goals. Healing provides the emotional clarity and mental space necessary to reconnect with what gives life meaning and purpose.

Setting New Goals for Personal Growth: Actionable Steps to Evolve After Healing

Once you've redefined your purpose, the next step is setting new goals that support your personal growth. Healing is not just about recovering from pain but also about evolving and growing into a more empowered version of yourself. Setting clear, achievable goals helps you build momentum and continue your journey forward.

David had spent years in therapy after recovering from a severe injury that upended his career as an athlete. After healing both physically and emotionally, David decided it was time to set new goals for himself. He realized that while he couldn't return to professional sports, he could use his experience to mentor young athletes. By setting a series of small goals, including coaching certifications and building connections with local sports organizations, David found a new path that allowed him to grow and contribute to others in a meaningful way.

Here are some actionable steps to set new goals for growth:

1. **Reflect on your values:** Now that you've healed, what matters most to you? Use these values to guide the goals you set for your future.

2. **Start small:** Begin with small, manageable goals that build confidence. For example, if you want to improve your physical health, start with a 10-minute daily exercise routine.

3. **Set measurable targets:** Make your goals specific and measurable, such as "I will read one personal development book per month," or "I will complete a 5K by the end of the year."

4. **Embrace learning:** Personal growth often requires acquiring new skills or knowledge. Commit to life-

long learning by attending workshops, reading, or finding a mentor.

According to a 2016 study in *Motivation and Emotion*, setting new goals after a period of healing contributes to long-term emotional stability and personal satisfaction. These goals provide structure, meaning, and a sense of forward movement.

Embracing Change: Using Your Newfound Courage to Navigate Future Challenges

Healing equips you with resilience and courage, tools that are essential for embracing change. Life is full of uncertainties and new challenges, but when you've worked through emotional pain, you become better prepared to face whatever comes next. The same courage that helped you heal is now available to help you embrace the inevitable changes life will bring.

Monica's experience exemplifies this. After surviving a difficult health crisis, she came out stronger and more self-assured. She no longer feared change because her healing journey had shown her that she was capable of navigating life's challenges.

When Monica was offered a promotion that required her to relocate to a new city, she saw it as an opportunity for growth rather than something to be feared. Her healing journey had taught her that change, while uncomfortable, often leads to personal transformation.

Research has shown that those who embrace change with a positive mindset are more likely to thrive in challenging situations. A 2020 study published in *Personality and Social Psychology Bulletin* found that emotional resilience gained from healing enhances adaptability and fosters a greater sense of self-efficacy. Embracing change becomes less daunting when you have already survived and grown from past challenges.

The Continuous Journey: Recognizing That Healing Is a Lifelong Process

Healing isn't something that happens overnight, nor is it a one-time event. It's a lifelong process that requires ongoing self-reflection, self-care, and growth. There will be times when old wounds resurface or new challenges emerge, but these moments are part of the continuous journey toward wholeness.

Aaron had overcome a traumatic childhood, finding peace through therapy and meditation. Yet, years later, when faced with the sudden loss of a loved one, old feelings of abandonment resurfaced. Instead of being discouraged, Aaron reminded himself that healing is a lifelong process. He returned to the practices that had helped him before—journaling, meditation, and seeking support from loved ones. Aaron understood that healing isn't linear, but it's always possible, as long as you're committed to the journey.

This concept is echoed in scientific literature. A 2017 study in *Trauma, Violence, & Abuse* emphasized that emotional healing is a cyclical process. The study highlighted the importance of ongoing emotional maintenance, including regular self-care, therapy, and reflection, as key components in maintaining emotional health over the long term.

Key Insights:

- Healing helps you rediscover your life's purpose, allowing you to redefine your path with clarity and intention.

- Setting new goals for personal growth is essential to evolve after healing. These goals should reflect your values and be actionable and measurable.

- Embracing change is easier with the resilience and courage gained from your healing journey, allowing you to face future challenges with confidence.

- Healing is a continuous, lifelong process that requires ongoing attention, reflection, and self-care.

Conclusion:

Moving forward with purpose after healing is a powerful and transformative experience. As you shed old emotional baggage, you make space for new opportunities, new goals, and a renewed sense of purpose. This chapter has explored how healing helps you redefine your life's path, the importance of setting new personal growth goals, embracing change, and understanding that healing is a lifelong journey. With each step forward, you move closer to a more fulfilling and authentic life, guided by purpose and resilience.

Resources:

1. Journal of Positive Psychology (2019). "Healing and Purpose: The Role of Emotional Recovery in Re-

defining Life Goals."

2. Motivation and Emotion (2016). "The Power of Goal Setting for Long-Term Emotional Stability and Growth."

3. Personality and Social Psychology Bulletin (2020). "Resilience and Adaptability: How Healing Fosters Courage in the Face of Change."

4. Trauma, Violence, & Abuse (2017). "The Lifelong Process of Healing: Insights into Emotional Recovery and Maintenance."

5. Dweck, C. S. (2006). *Mindset: The New Psychology of Success.*

CONCLUSION: YOUR COURAGE, YOUR HEALING

Celebrating Your Progress: Reflecting on the Transformation

Healing is a journey, and the fact that you've come this far is a testament to your courage, resilience, and determination. You've faced emotional wounds, battled fear, rebuilt trust, and cultivated self-compassion. Each of these steps has contributed to your transformation, shaping you into a stronger, wiser, and more empowered version of yourself. Take a moment to celebrate your progress—acknowledge the effort you've put in and the growth you've experienced.

Sarah, a woman who struggled with deep grief after the loss of her father, realized after years of reflection and self-work how far she had come. She learned to live with her loss, not by forgetting, but by integrating her grief into her life and allowing it to deepen her connection with others. Today, Sarah mentors those going through similar experiences, helping them to navigate their own grief journeys. Her progress is not just about overcoming pain but using it to foster deeper empathy and connection with others.

As you reflect on your own journey, recognize the transformation you've undergone. Every step, no matter how small, is part of a larger narrative of growth. You are no longer the person who first embarked on this path. You have evolved, healed, and continue to grow.

The Legacy of Resilience: Passing on the Gift of Courage to Others

One of the most beautiful outcomes of healing is the ability to pass on the lessons you've learned to others. Your resilience doesn't just benefit you—it has the potential to uplift and inspire those around you. Whether through mentoring, offering support, or simply being a living example of resilience, you have the ability to create a ripple effect that impacts the lives of others.

James had spent years struggling with addiction and the shame that accompanied it. After working through his emotional scars and overcoming his addiction, he dedicated himself to helping others on the same path. Today, James runs support groups for people in recovery, using his own story of courage and resilience to show others that healing is possible. His legacy is not just his own recovery but the courage he instills in those who follow in his footsteps.

Your courage and resilience are gifts that you can share with others. Whether it's friends, family, or even strangers, the strength you've developed through your healing journey can serve as a beacon of hope for those who need it most. By sharing your experiences, you contribute to a culture of healing and empowerment.

Living a Life of Purpose: Using Your Journey to Inspire and Uplift

As you move forward, your healing journey becomes a foundation for living a life of purpose. The challenges you've overcome have given you unique insights, empathy, and strength that can be channeled into meaningful pursuits. Whether your purpose involves helping others, pursuing personal passions, or creating a positive impact in your community, your journey has equipped you with the tools to live a purposeful life.

Lena, after healing from a difficult childhood marked by abuse, found her purpose in advocating for children's rights. She used her experiences to guide her in creating programs that offer support to children from difficult backgrounds, ensuring they have the resources she lacked. Lena's life of purpose was born from her healing, transforming her past pain into a source of strength and positive action.

Living with purpose doesn't always require grand gestures. It can be as simple as showing up for those around you, spreading kindness, or pursuing your passions with dedication. Your healing journey has made you stronger, more compassionate, and more equipped to inspire others by simply being who you are.

A Final Word of Encouragement: Reaffirming Your Ability to Thrive

You have shown immense courage in confronting your pain, facing your fears, and rebuilding your life. The journey hasn't been easy, but you've proven that you have the strength, resilience, and determination to thrive. Healing is not about reaching a final destination but continuing to grow, evolve, and face each new challenge with the knowledge that you can overcome it.

Remember, you are capable of thriving. No matter what life throws your way, you have the tools, the courage, and the wisdom to navigate it. Healing is a continuous process, but you have already shown that you have what it takes to keep moving forward.

So, take a deep breath. Reflect on how far you've come. And remember: the journey ahead is yours to shape, with courage guiding your way.

Key Insights:

- Celebrate the progress you've made—every step has contributed to your transformation.

- Your resilience can inspire and uplift others, creating a legacy of courage and hope.

- Use your healing journey to live a life of purpose, making a positive impact in whatever way resonates with you.

- You have the ability to thrive, no matter the challenges ahead. Your journey of healing has equipped you with the strength to continue growing and evolving.

MAY I ASK YOU FOR A SMALL FAVOR?

I want to express my sincere gratitude for choosing to invest your time in reading this book. Your decision to explore this work among countless others means a lot to me.

I hope that within these pages, you've discovered actionable insights that can enhance your daily life. Your journey doesn't have to end here, though.

May I kindly request an additional 30 seconds of your valuable time?

Sharing your thoughts about the book through a review would be immensely appreciated. Your review serves as a beacon, guiding other readers to take a chance on my books. It's a small gesture that carries significant weight in the world of authors.

To submit your review effortlessly, please click on the link below. It will take you directly to the book's review page:

"The Courage To Heal"

Alternatively, you can also find the "**Reviews Section**" of this book's page on Amazon.

Your review will require just a minute of your time but will make a monumental difference in helping me connect with a broader audience and I eagerly look forward to reading your review.

Once again, thank you for your unwavering support of my work.

DISCLAIMER

This book is for educational purposes only. Readers acknowledge that the author does not render legal, financial, medical, or professional advice. The content within this book has been derived from various sources. Please consult a licensed professional before attempting any techniques outlined in this book.

By reading this document, the reader agrees that under no circumstances is the author responsible for any direct or indirect losses incurred as a result of the use of the information contained within this document, including but not limited to errors, omissions, or inaccuracies.

Adherence to all applicable laws and regulations, including international, federal, state, and local governing professional licensing, business practices, advertising, and all other jurisdictions, is the sole responsibility of the purchaser or reader.

Neither the author nor the publisher assumes any responsibility or liability whatsoever on behalf of the purchaser or reader of these materials. Any perceived slight of any individual or organization is purely unintentional.